ALAN McWHIRR

ROMAN CRAFTS AND INDUSTRIES

D1070267

SHIRE ARCHAEOLOGY

Cover illustration
Reconstruction of a mosaicist's workshop
in the Corinium Museum, Cirencester.
(Copyright, Corinium Museum. Photograph, Rex Knight.)

Published by
SHIRE PUBLICATIONS LTD
Cromwell House, Church Street, Princes Risborough,
Aylesbury, Bucks, HP17 9AJ, UK.

Series Editor: James Dyer

ISBN 0 85263 594 X

First published 1982, reprinted 1988

Set by Avocet, Aylesbury, and printed in Great Britain by
C. I. Thomas & Sons (Haverfordwest) Ltd,
Press Buildings, Merlins Bridge, Haverfordwest.

Contents

List of illustrations

Preface

The coming of the Roman army to Britain had the effect of both stimulating existing crafts and introducing new ones. The troops had to be fed and supplied with equipment and their numbers gave rise to correspondingly large orders and hence mass production. The creation of cities and towns with regular markets along with improved communications meant that trade could be contemplated over a much wider area than before.

In recent years a number of people have made great strides in understanding Roman crafts, with the consequence that much more is known now than ten years ago. Although only an outline can be given in this book, it is hoped that it will be sufficient to indicate the wide range and great complexity of crafts that existed in Britain nearly two thousand years ago. A more detailed account is given in *Roman Crafts*, edited by D. Strong and D. Brown, a book which has been invaluable in the preparation of this work.

Nick Griffiths has drawn all the figures with the exception of the building from Itchingfield, which was done by Talbot Green. Several have been adapted from other people's illustrations and these have been duly acknowledged. Various museums have kindly provided photographs and the author is particularly grateful for the help received from Catherine Johns, Sue Read, Dennis Jackson, Mrs I. E. Shaw, Dr J. P. Wild, John Rhodes and David Viner. John Wacher kindly read an early version of the text and Helen McWhirr provided invaluable editorial assistance.

Plate 1. Gold buckle found in a hoard, along with eighty other gold and silver objects, at Thetford, Norfolk. (British Museum.)

1

Metals

Before the Roman invasion of Britain in AD 43 the native population was well versed in the techniques of extracting metals and of working them into quite sophisticated objects. Gold, silver, lead, tin, copper and iron were used in prehistoric times both on their own and occasionally as alloys. In the case of gold, silver and iron sufficient was being produced to create a surplus which was exported, as the philosopher and author Strabo tells us when writing about Britain before the conquest. With the coming of the Romans and the occupation of the country by the army it was essential to secure supplies of raw materials for repairing and replacing their equipment. The extraction and handling of lead, tin, copper and iron were most likely placed under military control to begin with. Similarly any supplies of gold or silver would initially have been commandeered for the imperial mints. Eventually during the four centuries of Roman rule some of these activities were handed back to private enterprise, but mostly on a concessionary basis – the state still took its tithe.

Gold

The only known Roman gold mine in Britain was at Dolaucothi, Dyfed, where remains can still be seen today, although not all are of Roman date (fig. 1). Originally the works consisted of both open-cast workings and mining galleries. There were two aqueducts which brought water to the site, to help to break down the rock and to wash the ores. One of these was 11 kilometres (6¾ miles) long and, it has been calculated, could deliver 13 million litres (2.9 million gallons) of water a day to the mine. As some of the galleries were 25 metres (82 feet) below ground, drainage was necessary and was carried out by a series of wooden waterwheels which raised the water from one level to another. Once the naturally occurring gold had been separated from other extraneous material it was melted and the liquid gold poured into moulds to form ingots, which were then either sent to official stores or sold to goldsmiths, whose presence has been attested in a number of towns in Roman Britain and at Dolaucothi itself. A goldsmith's workshop found at Verulamium was identified by the discovery of several small crucibles which had been used for heating gold. Another similar crucible was found in the market hall at Cirencester.

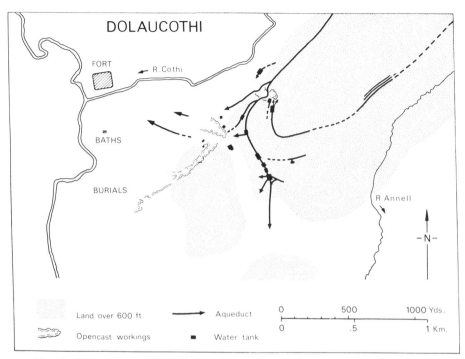

Fig. 1. Plan of Roman finds from Dolaucothi, Dyfed, associated with the extraction of gold. Two aqueducts brought water to the site from the north-east to break down the rock and wash the ores, which were obtained by open-cast workings as well as from mines. (N. A. Griffiths.)

There is evidence that gold was refined in London, for from the site that was later to become the Governor's palace have come two large gold-impregnated crucibles, three matching lids and pieces of baked clay which were used to seal these lids. A detailed analysis of these finds shows that the impure gold was heated in a crucible along with a mixture of brick dust and urine. Impurities were absorbed by the brick dust and attacked by the acid fumes from the urine leaving a pure molten gold, which could then be poured off. An iron punch bearing the letters *M.P.BR* – *Metalla Provinciae Britanniae* ('Mines of the province of Britain') – may have been used by an official who was responsible for refining and checking gold.

Jewellery was the main product of goldsmiths and many gold items have been found from all over Britain. Chain necklaces with gold fasteners seem to have been popular, as were rings, bracelets, earrings and pendants (plates 1 and 2). The great skill of the

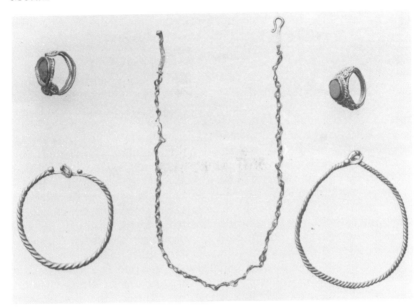

Plate 2 (above). A selection of gold jewellery including rings, bracelets and a necklace. (British Museum.)

Plate 3 (right). A late-Roman silver ingot found in Kent. It weighs 319.47 grams (11¼ ounces) and is 120 millimetres (4¾ inches) long. The inscription reads *EX OFF CVRMISSI*, which used to be interpreted as 'from the workshop of Curmissus'; however, some believe that it stands for *curator missionum*. (British Museum.)

goldsmith can be clearly seen in many of the items from the Thetford hoard and in particular the gold buckle (plate 1).

Silver

Ores of lead and silver are found together and consequently both metals have to be extracted in the same works. The stamps on lead pigs containing the abbreviated words *EX ARG* indicate that those pigs came from such an establishment (plates 6 and 7). Galena (lead sulphide) is the main ore of lead and is relatively easily converted into the metal by heating in a domestic charcoal or wood fire. If any silver ore is present an alloy of the two metals is produced by this process. To extract the silver, the alloy is reheated in a shallow bowl-shaped hearth lined with bone ash, and air is blown over the surface: this converts lead and other base metals to their oxides, which can be skimmed off, if they have not been absorbed by the bone ash, leaving behind pure silver. The temperature of about 1000-1100 C (1800-2000 F) needed for this technique, known as cupellation, could be achieved by using bellows on a charcoal or wood fire. Cupellation hearths have been found at Silchester, and these, along with an unfinished ring and droplets of silver, point to the presence of silversmiths working in the town.

Silver was used for jewellery, rings and bracelets being the most common items found, but it also seems to have been used extensively for religious plate, some pieces of which were associated with Christianity. Silver spoons sometimes bearing individual names and occasionally the chi-rho monogram may have been christening spoons. The recently discovered hoard from Water Newton, which consisted of ten objects, including a two-handled cup or 'chalice', three bowls, a shallow dish, a couple of flagons and a number of triangular plaques, may have come from a third- or early fourth-century church (plate 4). Several of the objects carried the Christian chi-rho monogram, and three vessels bore inscriptions which suggest that they were of religious significance. The collection of silver plate found at Mildenhall, Suffolk, included some quite remarkable pieces attesting the great skill of the contemporary silversmith (plate 5). However, these could have been made outside Britain and do not necessarily reflect the work of British craftsmen. One dish, measuring 600 millimetres (23½ inches) across and weighing 8.28 kilograms (18 pounds) was elaborately decorated with figures, some portraying the triumph of Bacchus over Hercules, and in the centre was the head of Neptune or Oceanus. There were also platters, bowls, goblets, spoons and a bowl with a lid displaying some decoration with niello inlay. The techniques used during the

Plate 4. Part of a late-Roman silver hoard found at Water Newton, Cambridgeshire, and which may have formed part of the plate from a church in the area. The two triangular plaques carry the chi-rho monogram, an indication of their Christian significance. (British Museum.)

Plate 5. Silver objects from Mildenhall, Suffolk. The great dish in the centre is 600 millimetres (23½ inches) in diameter and depicts the head of Neptune or Oceanus in the middle, around which are figures portraying the triumph of Bacchus over Hercules. (British Museum.)

Roman period differed little from those of today. Silver could be hammered into shape, and by careful polishing all traces of the hammer marks could be removed. Decoration was applied by a variety of techniques. Repoussé work involved hammering the back of the silver so that the pattern stood out in relief on the outside. Other techniques included engraving and chasing, which was done by hammering the surface of the silver with punches. A niello inlay was often employed; it had a shiny black finish and was made by heating silver sulphide.

By far the most dramatic discovery that showed the great skills of craftsmen in both gold and silver was made in 1979 when eighty-three pieces of late-Roman gold and silver were found at Thetford, Norfolk. The hoard included thirty-three silver spoons, three strainers and items of jewellery such as gold rings, bracelets and pendants. It must have been a jeweller's stock, which he had buried for safety, or loot.

Lead

Lead was produced at a number of centres in Britain, notably in the Mendips and Derbyshire, but also in the Shropshire border area, east Clwyd and Yorkshire. Before leaving the mines it was cast into inscribed moulds, many of which weighed in the region of 80 to 90 kilograms (175-200 pounds), and often stamped. These moulded inscriptions and the stamps give an insight into the organisation of the industry. Pigs from the Mendips dated to AD 49 show how quickly after the conquest the production of lead came under official control, and the discovery of such pigs at Southampton and St Valery-sur-Somme is a clear indication that they were being exported to the continent within a few years of the Roman army gaining control of southern England. Gradually the running of the leadworks was handed over to private enterprise, as the later stamps on the pigs indicate, and the works were leased to a company (*societas*). One company, which ran the Mendips works, stamped on its lead pigs the abbreviation *Soc No* or *Soc Novec*, which is short for *Societas Novaec*, the Novaec company (plate 7). The largest, if not the only, company which ran the Derbyshire works carried the title *Lutudarenses*, the name possibly being that of the locality where they operated (plate 6). The only mining settlement known in any detail is the one at Charterhouse in the Mendips, which consisted of a small town, an amphitheatre and a fort to house troops during the initial exploitation of the mines (fig. 2).

Lead was used extensively in the building trade for water pipes, bath linings, roofing and for water tanks or cisterns. Plumb-bobs

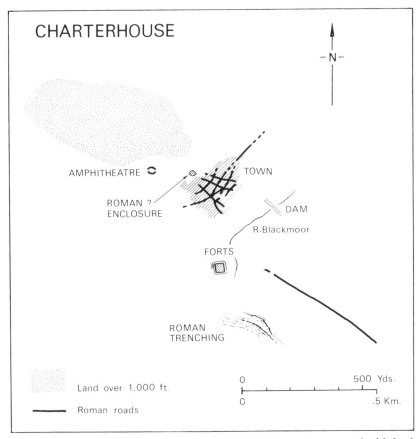

Fig. 2. Plan of Roman features at Charterhouse, Somerset, connected with lead mining. To begin with, these works were controlled by the army, but gradually they were handed over to private enterprise. An extensive civilian settlement gradually evolved with regularly laid-out streets and an amphitheatre. (N. A. Griffiths.)

and weights were made of lead as were some coffins and containers for cremated remains. By the late third century pewter, an alloy of tin and lead, was becoming increasingly important and many hoards of pewter have been found, including one from Icklingham, Suffolk, which comprised forty items.

The increased activity in the Cornish tin mines in the third and fourth centuries and the abundance of lead from the Mendips probably accounted for the development of the pewter industry in the West Country. Evidence for its production has come from

Lansdown near Bath, Camerton on the Fosse Way between the Mendips and Bath, and Nettleton Shrub, Wiltshire. Pewter was cast in stone moulds held together with iron clamps.

Tin

The major deposits of tin known to the Romans were in Devon and Cornwall and had been exploited long before the conquest. The ore, an oxide of tin, required a temperature of around 600 C (1100 F) to smelt it; so far no furnaces capable of carrying out this operation have been found. It could be found in stream beds where water-concentrated deposits, or *stream tin*, could be collected. Tin was

Plate 6 (below). Lead pig found at Hexgrave Park, Mansfield, Nottinghamshire, and carrying the inscription *C IVL PROTI BRIT LVT EX ARG*, showing that it originally came from the leadworks in Derbyshire whose name was probably *Lutudarensis*. This is abbreviated on the inscription to *Lut*. It is about 550 millimetres (22 inches) long. (British Museum.)

Plate 7 (bottom). Lead pig found at Syde just to the north of Cirencester, Gloucestershire. The inscription reads *IMP VESP AVG VIII BRIT EX ARG*, which dates it to AD 79. It also has *GPC* stamped on one end and *SOC NOVEC* on the side, standing for *Gaius Publius C (...)* and *Novaec Societas*, the Novaec Company which mined in the Mendips. It is 580 millimetres (22¾ inches) long and weighs 79 kilograms (174 pounds). (Corinium Museum.)

Plate 8 (left). Pewter ingot stamped with *SYAGRI* and the chi-rho monogram. Found in the Thames at Battersea, London. 380 millimetres (15 inches) in length. (British Museum.)
Plate 9 (right). Bronze jug found at Faversham, Kent. The decorated handle shows a figure of Diana. 190 millimetres (7½ inches) high. (British Museum.)

used mainly as an alloy with other metals: with lead to form pewter, and copper to give bronze.

Copper

Copper had been known for a long time in Britain and the Romans continued to work the main deposits in Cornwall, Shropshire, Wales and Anglesey. At Great Orme's Head near Llandudno there appears to have been a mining settlement, from which may have come the copper or bun ingots, some of which are inscribed. Other bun ingots have occurred in Anglesey, and one found at Aberffraw was stamped *SOCIO ROMAE-NATSOL*, a private firm.

Copper was rarely used on its own but was usually alloyed with tin or zinc to form bronze or brass. Objects of copper alloy are a common find on excavations of Roman sites, and many craftsmen must have been employed producing them. At Baldock some blanks which were to be made up into brooches have been found, whilst on the Isles of Scilly a workshop existed which specialised in enamelled bronze objects. At Catterick and Verulamium there were bronzesmiths making and selling their wares.

Bronze could be worked cold, as long as the composition of tin was kept below about thirteen per cent, to produce some of the smaller and uncomplicated objects, by hammering and turning on lathes. For cast bronze some lead was added, and so the composition of bronze objects varies, depending upon its method of production and the skill and experience of the craftsman.

Objects could be cast by one of two methods. For small objects the lost wax method was used. A model of the finished object was first made in wax and then coated with clay, or clay and sand. When this was heated the wax ran out, leaving a void in the clay the exact shape of the object. This void was then filled with liquid bronze and the whole thing allowed to cool. Finally the clay was broken away and the bronze object removed for cleaning and polishing. Larger objects were hollow cast, so that the final object was hollow inside rather than solid. Further additions of bronze could be made by using a solder of tin and lead; some jug handles are soldered in this way (plate 9).

Bronze could be decorated by a variety of techniques including carving on to the surface, the use of enamel, tinning or hammering into dies, and sometimes niello was used. This was a black decorative inlay, usually of copper and silver sulphides. Over ten thousand bronze brooches recorded in Britain exhibit many of the techniques described. Some were made by casting and others by forging, and a wide range of decoration is represented. Occasionally craftsmen made use of enamel, a vitreous substance fused to the metal. It was made by melting a soft glass with the addition of metallic oxides to produce the desired colour. The mixture was then ground to a powder and placed into cut-out areas of the metal object, the different colours being arranged to form the required pattern. It was then heated so that the powder melted and partly fused with the metal. Enamelling was not restricted to brooches, but was also used on seal boxes, rings, studs and skillet handles.

Many everyday articles were made from an alloy of copper and tin usually described as bronze; these include pins, needles, seal boxes, plates, skillets, fittings for furniture and harness fittings as well as the items of jewellery already mentioned such as rings, bracelets, brooches and necklaces. The Roman army also used bronze for

Plate 10. A selection of enamelled bronze objects including brooches, discs and studs. (British Museum.)

body armour, helmets, shield bosses and scabbards, and the soldier's diploma, which he was given on discharge, consisted of a pair of bronze plates on which were inscribed details of his career. More specialised bronze items include medical instruments and steelyards for weighing.

Iron

The occurrence of iron ore in Britain is widespread; it has been worked at one time or another in twenty-nine out of the forty-one English counties, although in Roman times the main centres of production were the Weald of Sussex and Kent, the Forest of Dean and the Northamptonshire and Lincolnshire region. It can be found in a variety of forms, the most common being the oxide, carbonate and sulphide of iron, of which the first two were the most widely used.

Iron ore was generally obtained by open-cast mining because of its easy availability, although at Lydney, Gloucestershire, in the Forest of Dean, underground galleries were dug. Some workings were controlled by the army and navy; at Corbridge, iron from the area around Risingham was worked by troops, and in the Weald several sites produced tiles stamped by the *Classis Britannica* (British fleet), implying some link with the navy. Elsewhere the scale of production ranged from quite small concerns having a single furnace operating to those with several furnaces capable of producing a steady supply of iron for local needs and for sale over a wider area. The reduction of ore requires heat and some form of chamber, or furnace, to contain the ore, and the presence of the correct gases.

First the ore was roasted in an open hearth using wood as a fuel, such as the examples found at Bardown, Sussex. When it was ready it was smelted in a furnace, of which there appear to be two main types, a non-slag-tapping furnace and a slag-tapping furnace (fig. 3). In Britain only the second type has been found and positively identified and it is usually referred to as a shaft furnace because of the cylindrical superstructure. The material from which these furnaces were made varies from one area to another, but clay was used when available and was considered to be particularly suitable. The cylindrical superstructure was probably formed by wrapping clay around a wooden former, possibly a tree trunk. Even in areas where stone was used to build the furnace, it was lined with clay. Once the furnace had been constructed, charcoal was placed in it and heated to a temperature of around 1300 C (2400 F), and then small amounts of iron ore and charcoal were added. Gradually, as

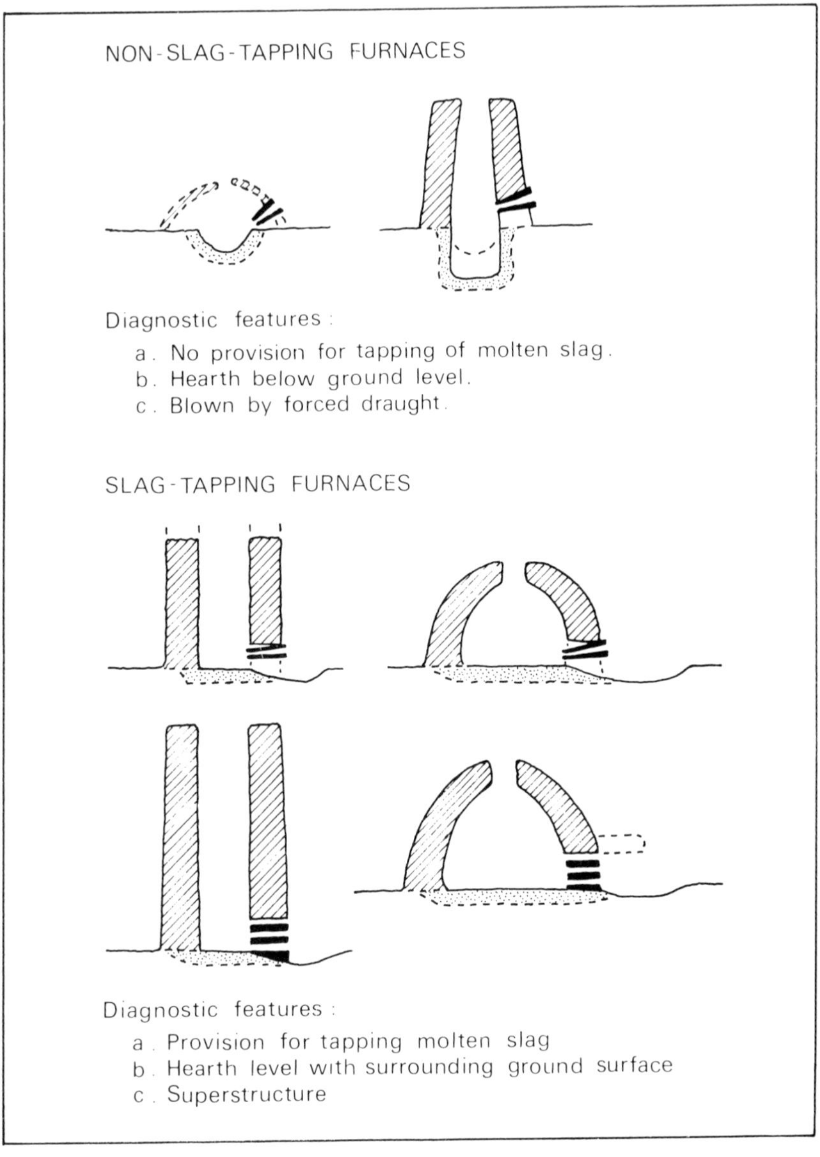

NON-SLAG-TAPPING FURNACES

Diagnostic features :

    a. No provision for tapping of molten slag.
    b. Hearth below ground level.
    c. Blown by forced draught.

SLAG-TAPPING FURNACES

Diagnostic features :

    a. Provision for tapping molten slag
    b. Hearth level with surrounding ground surface
    c. Superstructure

Fig. 3. Types of Roman furnaces in which iron was smelted. In Britain only slag-tapping furnaces have been identified, frequently referred to as shaft furnaces. (After H. Cleere.)

Plate 11. The remains of a jack-plane showing the iron sole and part of the iron casing. Found at Silchester in 1890 along with other woodworking tools, it is 135 millimetres (5¼ inches) long and 57 millimetres (2¼ inches) wide. (Reading Museum.)

Plate 12. Two hoards of blacksmith's tools were found at Silchester in 1890 and 1900 and some of these are shown here, including a sledge hammer, pliers, punches, drifts and nail-heading tools. (Reading Museum.)

Plate 13. A tombstone found at York showing a smith with a tunic draped over his left shoulder and an apron to protect his tunic. In his left hand he holds a pair of tongs in which he grips an object above an anvil. The right hand wields a hammer. (Yorkshire Museum.)

reduction of the ore proceeded, metallic iron began to form, as did a slag which was removed during smelting. Remaining behind after completion of the process was the bloom, which was removed from the furnace by tongs, either through the top of the shaft or through the furnace arch. It is not certain if steel, that is iron with carbon added, was made deliberately or whether it happened by chance, as for example in the blacksmith's forge where the iron could have accidentally picked up more carbon. The working of wrought iron by blacksmiths involved hammering the malleable red-hot metal into shape with tools very similar to those in use today, namely tongs, hammers, anvils and a variety of other equipment (plate 13).

Iron was widely used in Roman Britain. Many everyday tools of craftsmen or householders were made out of iron (plates 11 and 12). These included axes, hammers, chisels, saws and metal parts of wood planes. On the farm iron was used to make coulters, scythes and sickles. Soldiers carried daggers, swords and spears mainly made out of iron, and parts of some helmets were also of iron. In the building trade iron was used for hinges, locks and keys, to hold window glass in position and in the production of nails. Large iron beams, some weighing in the region of 250-300 kilograms (5-6 hundredweight), were used to support tanks of water over the furnaces of bath houses. Three have been found at Chedworth, one and a half at Catterick, one at the Jewry Wall site in Leicester and one, which was abandoned in the process of being made, at Corbridge.

2

Stone

Stone was little used for building in pre-Roman Britain, but gradually during the first century AD the demand for good-quality building stone increased, and quarries were opened up in areas that were geologically suitable and as conveniently situated as possible. Where such stone was not readily available builders had to use inferior materials, but even so they achieved high standards. Colchester was the first urban settlement to be established under Roman rule and, in the absence of stone which could be cut into regular building blocks, use was made of flint and brick, something totally new to the native population. The same circumstances applied at Verulamium. At Cirencester stone was at hand and when work started on the town's public buildings and streets, quarries were opened up to the west of the town to provide the huge quantities of stone that were required. In addition to stone, sand, gravel and lime were also necessary. Other towns soon needed supplies of stone, and consequently quarries began to open up all over Britain. At Leicester, for example, the local granite was used as well as stone brought from further afield, such as the millstone grit.

To begin with, stone was required for public buildings but as it came to be used more and more for houses and shops the demand was maintained. Stone defences were not generally constructed around towns until the third century, when a programme of wall building would have required enormous quantities of stone. At Cirencester, Mr Wacher has calculated that 84,000 cubic metres (3 million cubic feet) of masonry were needed for its town wall, and that every time the streets were relaid 11,000 cubic metres (400,000 cubic feet) of gravel or stone rubble were used. The quarries to the west of the town no doubt provided the bulk of what was required, but other sources in the neighbourhood were brought into operation to maintain supplies and to serve the needs of a growing number of villa owners who were now using stone for their buildings. For specific tasks some types of stone were better suited than others. Purbeck marble from Dorset was used for inscriptions at Chichester and Verulamium as well as for architectural purposes at many other settlements. On occasions stone was imported; many of the querns used in Britain were made of Niedermendig lava from Andenach, and marble from the Mediterranean adorned many a building of Roman Britain.

Details of quarrying techniques are hard to come by because the same areas were worked in post-Roman times, thus removing all traces of earlier activity. Several inscriptions from the region of Hadrian's Wall have been found in quarries and show the involvement of the army in extracting stone for this great defensive wall. Wedge holes have been noted at the sandstone quarry on Barcombe Down above Vindolanda, at Limestone Corner, Hadrian's Wall, and at Cirencester, where a Roman quarry face has been found and examined in detail. All show a technique, well known from elsewhere in the Empire, of splitting blocks of stone from their bed by driving a line of wedges either vertically or, as seems to be the case at Cirencester, horizontally as well.

Once blocks of stone had been hewn from the bed rock they were trimmed or dressed at the quarry to avoid transporting the unnecessary surplus. The smaller pieces of stone which resulted could be collected together and used for a number of purposes, such as road surfacing. The tools which were available to the cutters included a pick or pick hammer, an axe and adze for direct action on the stone, or a mallet to be used in conjunction with a point, drove or claw chisel (fig. 4). These could also be used to execute ornamental details on architectural pieces, although a wider range of chisels was available and a drill was sometimes used. One of the most common features of Roman building was the use of the column, and many of those found show clear evidence of having been turned on a lathe. Two types of lathe have been postulated: one on which the column was turned by hand from one end (end drive), and another where the column was rotated by means of a rope around its shaft, which in turn was linked to a large stone flywheel turned by hand (lateral drive – fig. 5).

When a stone suitable for roofing was found it was traded more widely than was the custom with the more common building materials. This can be illustrated in a number of areas. In the Cotswolds the local limestone was used, but in some places there was a preference for sandstone roof slates brought in from the Forest of Dean, a distance approaching 50 kilometres (30 miles). Collyweston slates from Rutland also had a wide distribution, but perhaps the clearest example of the wide distribution of a roofing material comes from the East Midlands, where Swithland slate, found only in one place 10 kilometres (6 miles) north-west of Leicester, has occurred on Roman buildings at many sites, including High Cross, Sapperton, Ancaster and Littlechester outside Leicestershire. The most distant sites on which it has been found are Norton Disney, near Lincoln, and Irchester, both being about 65 kilometres (40

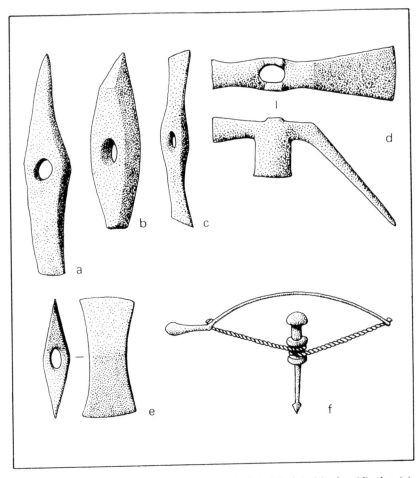

Fig. 4. A selection of Roman mason's tools: (a) pick, (b) pick, (c) adze, (d) adze, (e) axe, (f) drill. (After T. F. C. Blagg.)

miles) from the quarries. Although water transport on the rivers Soar, Trent and Derwent could have been used to move slate to some of these sites, it must have travelled by road to settlements east of Leicester such as Irchester.

Stone roofing 'slates' in the Roman period were diamond-shaped and fixed to the roof timbers by iron nails through a hole in the top of the slate. As in the medieval period, the slates may have been graduated in size with small ones at the ridge and larger ones

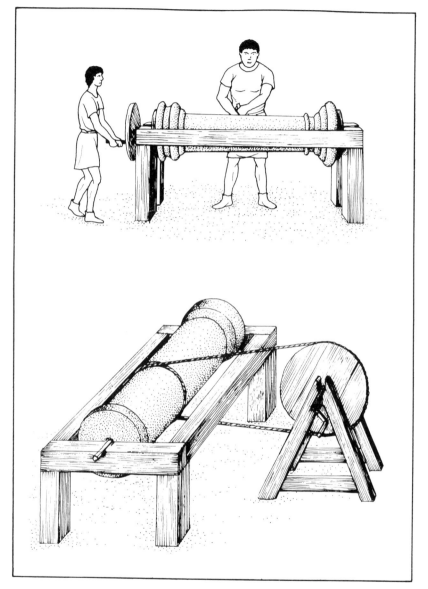

Fig. 5. Two suggested methods for turning heavy stone columns. Above, the power is provided by hand to the end of the column whilst, below, the column is turned by means of a rope attached to a flywheel. (After T. F. C. Blagg.)

Fig. 6. Stone was frequently used as a roof covering when available locally, and this reconstruction by Nick Griffiths is based on a finial found at Rockbourne, Hampshire, and stone tiles from Winchester. (N. A. Griffiths.)

towards the eaves. At Kingscote, Gloucestershire, specially made ridge stones have been found looking like upturned gutter stones, whilst on other sites excavators believe that the baked clay *imbrex* tile was used along the ridge. Occasionally stone roof finials decorated these buildings (fig. 6).

Apart from the building trade stone found many other applications. Tombstones set up to the memory of the dead occur early in the Roman occupation of Britain, as many were erected to

Fig. 7. Stone slabs decorated with chip carving along their edge have often been found in association with short columns, and it seems most likely that they were stone tables. (N. A. Griffiths.)

Plate 14. A sculptor who worked in Cirencester and Bath is recorded on this inscription from Bath. His name was *Sulinus*, which suggests that he was born in Bath and named after *Sulis*. (Bath Museum.)

soldiers. Such headstones often exhibit elaborate details and were probably carved by army personnel attached to the unit to which the deceased belonged. Gradually, however, the technique of carving letters and figured scenes was passed on to native craftsmen, who in their turn became the stonemasons responsible for carving civilian tombstones.

Altars in temples and private houses were made from stone, as were the many sculptured pieces of a religious significance. Those responsible for them are not always anonymous and from Bath come two inscriptions referring to stonemasons: the first, a dedication slab, records a mason named Priscus, who is described as a tribesman of the Carnutes, a tribe centred on Chartres; the second records a sculptor by the name of Sulinus, who is also mentioned on an inscription from Cirencester and whose name suggests that he was born in Bath (*Aquae Sulis*) (plate 14). A delightful gabled panel from Bisley, Gloucestershire, where Romulus is shown in the guise of Mars, carries an inscription showing that it was carved by Juventinus (plate 15).

Some items of furniture were made from stone, the commonest of which was a small side-table. The top was either rectangular or bow-

Plate 15. A votive tablet found near Bisley, Gloucestershire, showing Romulus in the guise of Mars. The importance of this piece is the inscription carved on the inside of the gabled niche, which says that 'Juventinus made it', giving us the name of another sculptor who worked in that area (see plate 14). (Gloucester Museum.)

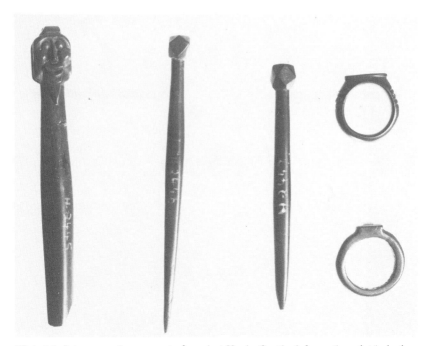

Plate 16. Jet personal ornaments found at York. On the left are three jet hairpins, the centre one of which is 105 millimetres (4¼ inches) long, and on the right two jet finger rings. (Yorkshire Museum.)

fronted in shape and three sides were decorated by chip carving, the whole being supported by a single dwarf column, with the plain edge of the top against the wall (fig. 7). Tables were also made out of Kimmeridge shale from the Dorset coast and shale table legs have been found over quite a wide area. Shale table tops are less common but have been found at Caerwent and Silchester. The legs and tops were joined together by a mortice and tenon joint. Kimmeridge shale was also used for jewellery, as was jet from Whitby in North Yorkshire. The discovery of worked blocks of jet in York indicates that workshops once existed in the city. Jet was used for carved hairpins, finger rings, bracelets, bead necklaces, bangles and pendants (plate 16).

Other materials extracted from the ground and used during the Roman period include coal, which has been found on military and civilian sites. Its occurrence on several farms in Gloucestershire points to its having been mined in the Forest of Dean. The Somerset and Clwyd coalfields, among many others, were also exploited.

Fig. 8. A reconstruction of the lower part of a square or rectangular kiln of the sort used for firing tile and brick, although some kilns of this shape were also used for pottery. The side walls would have stood much higher than shown in the drawing. (N. A. Griffiths.)

Plate 17. A Roman brick found at Cirencester bearing the stamp *Arveri*, showing that *Arverus* was in some way involved in brickmaking in the Cotswolds. The frame of the stamp measures approximately 60 by 20 millimetres (2½ inches by ¾ inch).(Cirencester Excavation Committee.)

3

Brick, tile and pottery

Brick and tile

Although clay had long been worked for pottery making in pre-Roman Britain, the use of it to make bricks was totally unknown. The techniques for producing and firing brick and tile were introduced by the Roman soldiers, who required them for building their forts and fortresses; one of the earliest sites where the extensive use of brick and tile can be seen is Exeter, where a fortress for the Second Legion was constructed between AD 55 and 60. The military craftsmen would soon have been able to pass on their skills to those native workers who were used to handling clay for making pottery; gradually they in turn added brick and tile production to their activities. With the founding of towns and construction of villas there were considerable profits to be gained from this craft.

Clay suitable for making brick is to be found over a wide area, although for quality products some clays are better than others. It was dug in the autumn and allowed to weather over the winter. With the coming of spring further treatment was carried out, including the removal of stones, which could be accomplished by puddling the clay with bare feet. Once the clay was ready, the brick caster set up his work bench and erected some primitive shelter, probably made out of branches, and began to mould bricks. The finished articles were taken to a drying area and allowed to harden before being stacked in a kiln and eventually fired.

Various graffiti on brick indicate that production was a seasonal operation, probably extending from April to September, although it might start earlier or finish later if the weather were suitable. Brick kilns have been found in many parts of Britain. They were rectangular or square in plan, there being no circular kilns in Britain used for firing brick, such as those in Italy and Sicily. A combustion chamber was constructed below ground which contained a series of closely spaced walls, supporting the oven floor above (fig. 8). The kiln was heated by a fire which was controlled from a stokehole, and the hot air was drawn through a central flue in the combustion chamber, or, in at least two cases, by double parallel flues, through vents in the oven floor into the kiln. The side walls of the combustion chamber were taken above the level of the oven floor to provide side walls to the kiln itself. As these kilns had to be loaded by passing

Plate 18. A tile and brick kiln during the course of excavation at Heighington, Lincolnshire. Both ranging poles are marked in half metres. (H. N. Hawley.)

objects over these side walls, rather than through an entrance left in one of the walls, the roofing would have been temporary, perhaps turves, straw or waste brick and tile. The fuel was, in most cases, wood or charcoal, although straw could have been used; indeed the choice of fuel dictated the design of the kiln, affecting the length of the main central flue in the combustion chamber. A temperature of about 1000 C (1800 F) was reached and in an oxidising atmosphere the familiar red-coloured brick and tile were produced. After cooling, the kiln was unloaded and the products were stored until required (plate 18).

Occasionally during their manufacture some tiles were stamped or had finger marks made across them, or on occasions both, and a study of these is providing information about the organisation of the industry. The earliest stamped tiles are two from Silchester which were stamped when Nero was emperor, that is between AD 54 and 68, and simply contain part of his official title *NER CL CAE AVG GER*. Stamped tiles from London bearing the letters *PPBRLON* or *PRBRLON* or *PPRBR* may also be late first century in date. The letters *PBRLON* clearly stand for *Provinciae Britanniae Londinii*, which means 'of the province of Britain in London'. The first *P* most likely represents the word *Procurator*, an official who was based in London.

Gloucester also had a municipal tileworks by the first quarter of the second century AD and stamped many of its products with the letters *RPG* (*Rei Publicae Glevensium*), occasionally followed by the name of a person, almost certainly a magistrate who was responsible for the city's brickyards. Other brickmakers in the Cotswolds followed this pattern of stamping tile and brick.

At Lincoln there have been found over forty tiles stamped *LVLA*, *LVLD, LVLE* and *LVL*, whereas from the rest of Britain the stamps only occur in ones or twos. From Colchester comes a stamp *LLS*, from London *SCM*, from Alcester *TCD* and from Wroxeter three *LCM*. The villa at Crookhorn, Hampshire, has tiles stamped *TIFR*, and there are some from Park Street with the letter *M* inscribed. It is now generally assumed that these groups of letters represent a shorthand form of a person's name, as is the case with some examples which are written out more extensively; for example, *ARVERI* and *IVC DIGNI* must represent the names *Arverus* and *Iucundus Dignus* (plate 17). Apart from in the Cotswolds the practice of stamping civilian tiles was not common in Britain, which contrasts with military practice from the second century onwards. Both the legions and auxiliary units stamped many of their tiles, as did bases connected with the British fleet, where hundreds of tiles stamped *CLBR* (*Classis Britannicus*) have been found.

Some bricks and tiles were marked by fingers, and these marks have been referred to as 'signatures' by some people, although their exact significance is unknown. Likewise cuts on the edge of tile and brick resembling Roman numerals may have been tally marks.

One of the most common uses for these clay products was in roofing. Roofs were made from two types of tile, a flat one with flanges (*tegula*) and a curved tile (*imbrex*) which fitted over the two flanges of adjacent *tegulae* (see fig. 9). *Tegulae* were made to fit into each other and overlap, thus forming a continuous surface on the roof. As the pitch of such roofs was probably between 20 and 30 degrees it would not have been necessary to nail every *tegula*. On some occasions the end of a line of *imbrices* was marked with a decorated plaque or antefix made from a mould. The ridge may have been formed by a line of ordinary *imbrices*; the tile from Canterbury with cut-out sections on each side has been claimed as a ridge tile, but it is the only example known and the cut-out portions are too close to fit over the raised sides on *tegulae*, and so it cannot be considered as a typical ridge tile.

Brick was used in walls and for arches, when good-quality stone

Fig. 9. Tiles made from clay and baked in kilns as shown in fig. 8 were commonplace in the Roman world, and this reconstruction shows how the different shaped tiles were used on a roof. The individual tiles are shown on fig. 10. (N. A. Griffiths.)

was not available, and in the construction of baths and heated rooms (hypocausts). In such rooms floors were supported on pillars of tile or stone, and flues were constructed in the walls of the room to allow the hot air and combustion gases to flow through the building. Wall flues were made from what are generally referred to as box-flue tiles (fig. 10), which were set into the wall and subsequently plastered over. To make the plaster adhere to the smooth tile surfaces they were either scored with a comb or decorated by using a roller, which created a pattern in relief (fig. 10).

There are many examples of graffiti on brick and tile, executed when the tile was still wet, presumably by people working in the

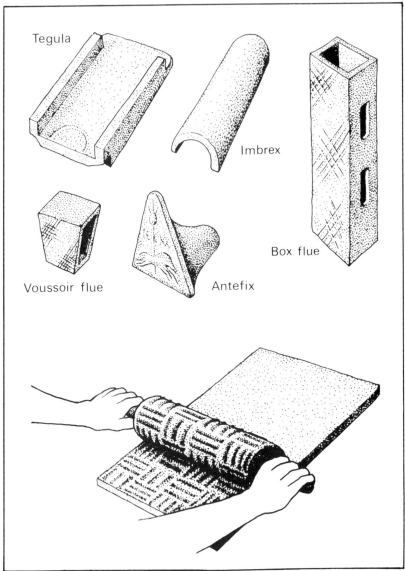

Fig. 10. Selection of tiles which were used in Roman buildings. The *tegula, imbrex* and *antefix* were used on roofs (fig. 9) and the box-flue tiles were recessed into walls one above the other to act as flues. The voussoir may also have been used to carry hot air around buildings, or alternatively it may have been a constructional device to reduce the weight of arches of vaults. Some tiles had impressions made on their surfaces by a cylindrical roller so that plaster would key to them securely. (N. A. Griffiths.)

1. Weathered clay brought up to work-shop's claystore

2. Clay transferred to pugging pit, as required

3. Pugged clay distributed to tile-makers working beside gangway

4. Tiles produced taken along gangway and out on to drying floor

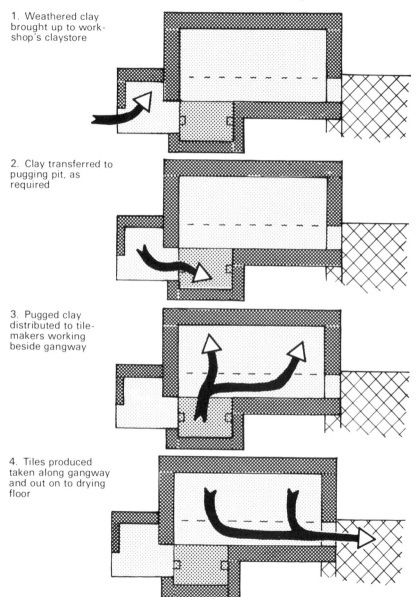

Fig. 11. A building excavated at Itchingfield, West Sussex, has been interpreted as a tilemakers' workshop and this diagram illustrates how it was probably used. (Talbot Green.)

brickyards. A box-flue tile from Leicester records that 'Primus had made ten' and one from Silchester states that 'Clementinus made this box-tile'. Several tiles have numbers on them which presumably record a total; a worker from the Silchester region, however, seems not to have bothered with the exact number, but simply recorded '*Satis*' – enough! One tile worker in London, upset by the activities of one Austalis, wrote on an unfired brick: 'Austalis has been going off by himself every day these last thirteen days!'

Brickmaking in Roman Britain was organised in a variety of ways, ranging from a single clamp or kiln supplying the needs of a household, to much larger concerns providing the cities with huge quantities of their products. The army had its own brickworks, and although the organisation of them was governed by military codes of practice and discipline, the technique was the same as in the civilian brickworks. The supply depot of the Twentieth Legion, which was based at Chester, covered some 20 acres (8 hectares) at Holt on the banks of the river Dee and was responsible for making tile, brick and pottery, much of which found its way to Chester. The most impressive structure at Holt was the bank of six kilns, all serviced from a single stoking area, which could have been fired in rotation, thus providing a continuous supply of brick when the occasion demanded. In Cumbria another group of kilns built by auxiliary units of the army has been found at Brampton, and many more such army brickworks must have existed. Groups of civilian tile kilns are known from Canterbury, Colchester, north-east Warwickshire and, perhaps the largest so far recognised, at Minety, Wiltshire, which supplied the second largest town in Roman Britain at Cirencester. Here some ten kilns are suspected, not, as at Holt, in a group, but scattered over a much wider area, perhaps indicating different concerns all working in the same brickfield rather than one large factory under single ownership.

Many of the buildings associated with brickmaking were probably very primitive in their construction. For making, drying and storing the bricks and tiles, simple wooden structures would have sufficed, and even the living quarters of larger works may not have been very impressive. One building, which has been interpreted as a tilemakers' workshop, was excavated at Itchingfield, West Sussex, and contained a clay store, a pugging pit, a work area and an external yard for drying (fig. 11).

Pottery

Unlike brick and tile, there was a long tradition of pottery making in Britain before AD 43, but with the coming of the Roman army

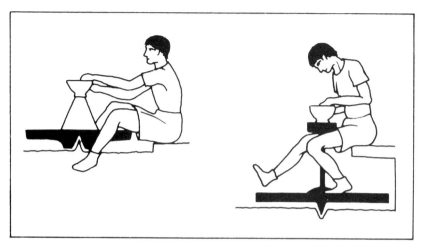

Fig. 12. Most of the Roman pottery made in Britain was thrown on a wheel which was probably turned by kicking a heavy flywheel such as the one illustrated in plate 32. (N. A. Griffiths.)

new forms were required and there was a sudden increase in demand. This was met to some extent by the native potters, but it appears that, to begin with, some immigrant craftsmen came over in the wake of the army. However, native craftsmen would not have been slow to react to the large market for their products and no doubt gradually began to undertake contract work for the army. Large civilian potteries emerged, centred in areas of good-quality clay, and there were many local potters supplying the needs of people in quite confined areas. A number of the techniques employed in pottery making were similar to those used in producing brick and tile, but for a more detailed study of Roman pottery the reader is referred to a companion volume in this series, *Pottery in Roman Britain* by Vivien G. Swan (fig. 12 and plate 32).

4

Textiles and leather

The bulk of the population in Roman Britain worked on the land as part of an enormous agricultural industry. Farming was based on a mixed economy, although, as today, in some parts of Britain climatic conditions and the terrain did not favour arable farming and so sheep and cattle predominated. The main rural crafts for which we have any evidence are concerned with textiles and leather.

Textiles

There are three basic processes in textile production: preparation of the fibre, spinning and weaving. Occasionally two other crafts may have been involved: dyeing and finishing (fulling). Wool was the main textile fibre used in the Roman period although flax and hemp occurred occasionally, there being quite a number of linen items from Britain. The source of the wool was two breeds of sheep: a small animal resembling the modern Soay sheep of St Kilda, which had a brown fleece, and an improved breed of Soay sheep which had a finer and normally white fleece. It was usual to shear sheep in the early summer with iron shears not unlike those used today, and sometimes the wool was then dyed 'in the fleece'. Plucking was also employed to remove the wool. With longer-stapled wools it was necessary to remove short fibres by using a flat iron comb with long teeth.

The fibre was now ready for spinning and this was carried out using basically two implements, the distaff and the handspindle. The former was simply a short forked stick, the prongs of which supported the mass of fibres to be spun. The handspindle was a narrow rod made out of bone or wood, thicker towards the lower end to hold fast the spindle whorl, which gave the spindle momentum when rotated (plates 19 and 20). Spindle whorls made from stone or pottery are frequently encountered during excavations, whereas the shank of the spindle, being made mainly from wood or bone, rarely survives.

The spun thread was then presumably wound into a ball for weaving. Although no actual looms survive there are representations in various works of art and from these and from the woven fabric itself it is possible to work out which sort were used. There were probably three types of loom in use in the Roman world, although

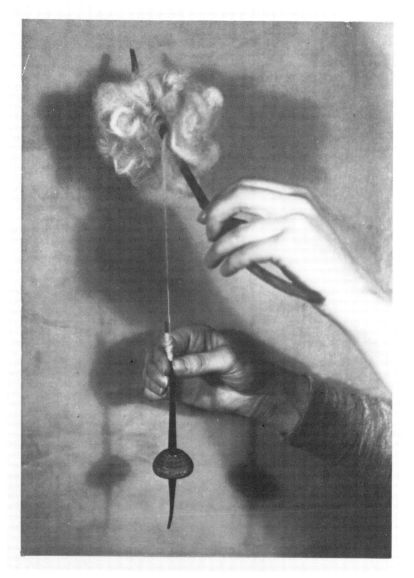

Plate 19. The use of a handspindle for spinning wool. The rod, or spindle, was usually made out of wood or bone, and the whorl at the lower end of stone or pottery. (Museum of London.)

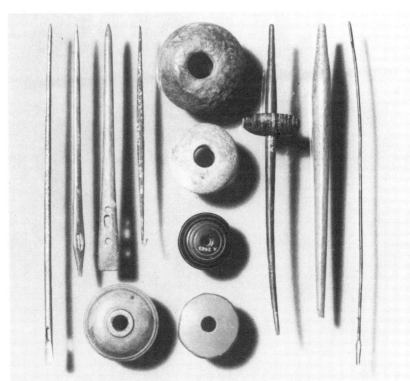

Plate 20. A selection of needles, spindles and whorls. (Museum of London.)

the third had a very limited geographical distribution. The two most common looms were the warp-weighted vertical loom and the two-beam loom; there is little evidence of the horizontal loom in the western provinces at all. Decorated or corded bands and borders could be made by tablet weaving, which involved the use of triangular or square plaques of bone, or by using a rigid heddle or a heddle frame (fig. 13).

It was usual to dye the fibre immediately after it had been produced, rather than the woven cloth, and for this purpose vegetable dyes, together with a mordant such as alum or salts of iron to make the dye take, were the most common. The fuller finished cloth by treading it in a tub of water containing a solution of fuller's earth or decayed urine, which removed excess grease and dirt. Sulphur was sometimes used to bleach wool cloth.

Some of the articles made from British wool were so well known throughout the Roman world that when Diocletian issued his price-

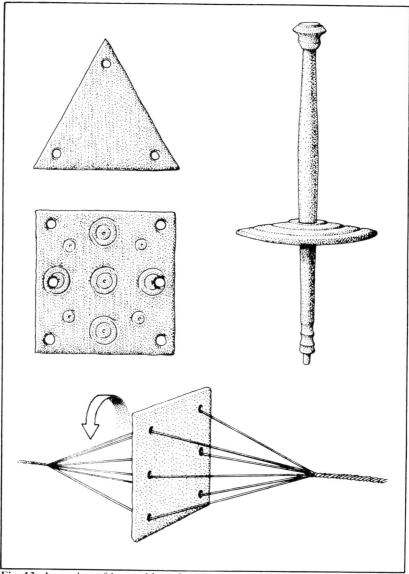

Fig. 13. A number of bone objects found on excavations have been identified as tablets used in weaving and they are usually triangular or square in shape. On the right of the figure is a spindle with weight attached (whorl) used in spinning. The spindles are usually made of bone or wood, and the whorls of stone or pottery. (N. A. Griffiths.)

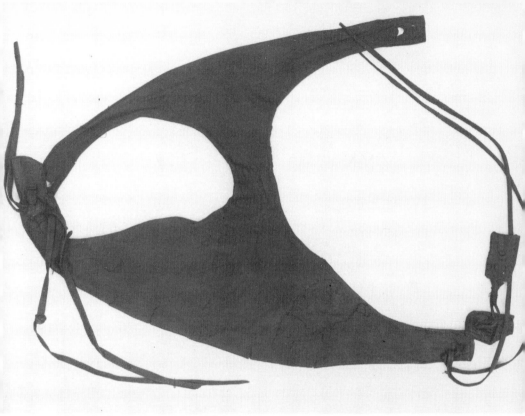

Plate 21. Leather trunks or 'bikini' of a young girl acrobat or dancer that were found in a first-century AD well in London. One side was still fastened with a granny knot. (Museum of London.)

fixing edict in AD 301 two of them were included. One was a hooded cloak not unlike a modern duffel coat and known as the *birrus Britannicus*, and the other a woollen rug which could be used on saddles or couches and which was referred to as the *tapete Britannicum*. Sculptured tombstones often show the deceased wearing items of clothing. For example, the first-century AD tombstone erected to Philus after he died in Cirencester shows him wearing a cape with a detached hood, but we cannot be certain whether this was made in the Cotswolds from local wool or whether Philus brought it with him from his homeland in Gaul.

Leather

Another major product from the farms of Roman Britain was hides, which could be processed into leather and then worked by skilled craftsmen into a wide range of articles including shoes, boots, sandals, tents, shields, items of clothing, bags, buckets, jugs, workmen's aprons, items of uniform and so on (plates 21 and 22).

Hides are converted into leather by a series of processes generally

Plate 22. A leather shoe from the Walbrook, London, measuring 270 millimetres (10¾ inches) in length. The overall triangular decoration appears to have been cut with a knife. (Museum of London.)

known as *tanning*; there are a variety of such processes, the choice of method depending upon the characteristics required in the finished product. First it was necessary to treat the hide to prevent damage from bacteria before it could be tanned, and this was often done by salting. Tanning could then be accomplished by using either tannin present in organic matter such as wood and bark or a solution of alum and salt. This converted the raw hide to a material which did not decay and which could be wetted and dried without adverse effects and generally be made more usable. The bulk of leather used in Roman Britain came from the ox or the cow although goat was occasionally used. The final appearance of the leather could be altered by staining, hammering or rolling, before cutting, stitching or moulding into the final product.

5
Glass

Glass was used in Roman Britain for a wide variety of vessels (plate 23) and for windows. It was produced by fusing silica (sand), soda and lime and there were probably three distinct stages in the production. To begin with, the mixture was heated either in a separate furnace or in the cooler part of the melting furnace to drive off some of the impurities and to lower the temperature required for fusion, a process known as *fritting*. Then the mixture was heated to about 1100-1200 C (2000-2200 F) in a fireclay crucible, where glass in a molten state was produced. This could then be used to make vessels by mould blowing or free blowing. Finally the vessels were annealed, or slowly cooled, in special annealing ovens.

Excavations at Wilderspool, Cheshire, have revealed some evidence for glassmaking. An oval furnace contained fritted glass, fragments of glass rod, crucibles and glass vessels, indicating that it was used for fritting and melting glass. A number of other structures found at this industrial complex have also been interpreted as part of the glassmaking process. There is also evidence of glass production from Colchester, Caistor-by-Norwich, Wroxeter, Silchester and Leicester.

The majority of glass vessels found in Britain were blown using long iron tubes or blowing irons probably about 1.2 metres (4 feet) long. The product, in the absence of any additional substances, was

Plate 23. A collection of glass vessels from Burgh Castle, Norfolk. The example on the left is about 100 millimetres (4 inches) high. (British Museum.)

bluish-green in colour, but this could be altered by adding metal oxides to produce a range of coloured glass. In addition to the blowing irons the glassworker required a pair of shears, pincers and a marver block on which to roll out and shape the glass before blowing. Limestone slabs found in association with the Wilderspool glass furnaces have been identified as such blocks.

Some glass vessels were made by blowing into a mould, sometimes decorated, and this was the usual method for making square bottles. Glass could be decorated when hot or cold. When hot the glass could be tooled with pincers or have blobs of glass added, thus producing quite sophisticated and sometimes coloured effects. Cold glass could be decorated in two ways: painting, and wheel cutting and engraving.

Window glass is frequently found on Roman sites in Britain and, to begin with, may have been made by casting the glass on sanded surfaces in moulds; later, however, it appears that panes were produced by blowing a cylindrical bottle in a mould, which was then cut open with shears and rolled out to give a flat pane of glass.

Fig. 14. A variety of locks and keys were used in Roman Britain; these were invariably made from iron. This example could have chains fitted to either end and act as a sort of padlock. (N. A. Griffiths.)

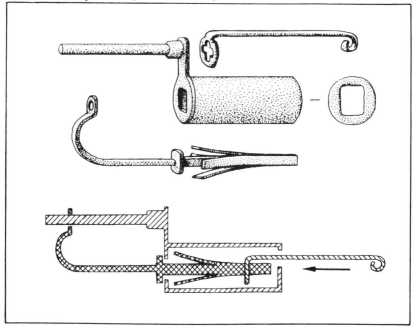

6

Other crafts

The crafts which existed in Roman Britain were many and varied; a few have already been discussed in detail, but it now remains to draw attention to some of the remainder. As well as producing textiles and leather, farmers were occupied in making cheese and possibly in keeping bees for honey. Trees from their estates were used for timber in the building trade, in which a number of craftsmen were employed, including masons, plumbers, glaziers, joiners, locksmiths, mosaicists, wall decorators and many others.

The skill of carpenters and joiners can be seen in the many examples of wooden products that have been found, ranging from quite small items to the wooden bridge discovered at Aldwincle (plates 26 and 27). Wood was also used for carts, barrels (plate 25), wheels and axles, the drainage wheel from the Dolaucothi gold mine, quays such as those found in London, and for boats. Two hoards of ironwork found at Silchester (which include chisels, gauges, saws, hammers and a jack-plane) indicate the range of woodworking tools available to the craftsmen of Roman Britain (plate 11).

The use of timber in building involved the skills of other craftsmen. Nails were used extensively and ranged in size from 20 millimetres to around 300 millimetres (¾ inch to 1 foot); windows required an iron grille; doors needed hinges, bolts and locks. Locks and keys were quite sophisticated and there was even a form of padlock (fig. 14).

Animal bone found a wide range of uses, for example in making tablets for weaving, rings, bracelets, hairpins, spoons, gaming counters, knife handles and dice (plate 31). Whether special craftsmen working solely in bone set up on their own is not known, but perhaps it is more likely that jewellers, weavers and others made the bone items they needed themselves. Hinges for cupboards, chests and boxes were also frequently made of bone (figs. 15 and 16).

Public buildings, shops and houses were decorated internally with mosaic floors, painted walls and ceilings, and occasionally stucco. Roman mosaics are dealt with fully in a companion volume in this series, *Romano-British Mosaics* by Peter Johnson, and so only a few words are needed here (plate 34). The *tesserae* from which they were constructed were of stone, though brick, glass and even samian

Plate 24. Reconstruction of a Roman carpenter's bench as displayed in the Museum of London. (Museum of London.)

Plate 25. Three wooden barrels photographed during the course of nineteenth-century excavations at Silchester. They were made from silver fir and were probably used to bring wine into Britain. (Reading Museum.)

Plate 26. Timbers of a Roman bridge exposed during the extraction of gravel at Aldwincle, Northamptonshire. These timbers were part of the bridge abutment. (D. A. Jackson.)

Plate 27 (above). Constructional details of the timbers used in the Roman bridge at Aldwincle, Northamptonshire. (D. A. Jackson.)

Plate 28 (left). Stave-built bucket found at Silchester and probably made of oak. (Reading Museum.)

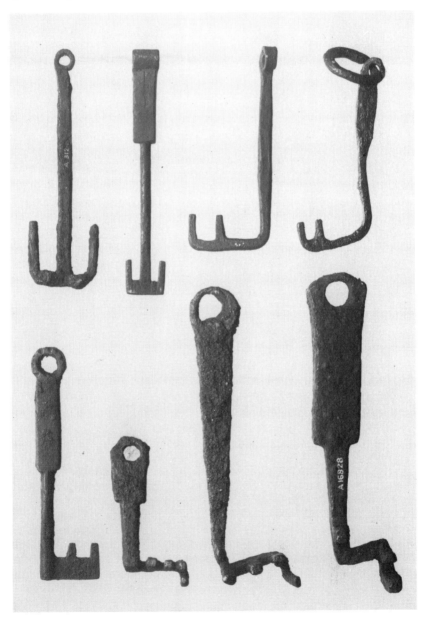

Plate 29. A selection of iron keys. (Museum of London.)

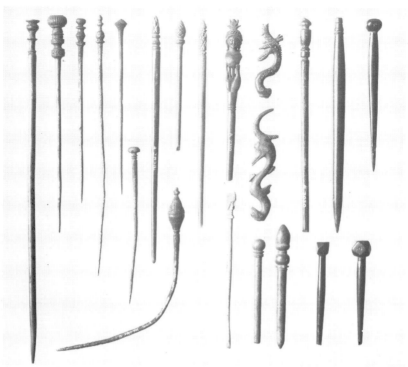

Plate 30. Pins made from bronze, bone and jet, the majority of which were used as hairpins. (Museum of London.)

pottery were sometimes used. Guide lines have been found underneath mosaic floors, showing that some were laid directly into the room, but it is also likely that sections of floors were made in workshops and brought to the building as a prefabricated unit. The skill of a mosaicist can be seen in the Woodchester Orpheus pavement, which is nearly 15 metres (50 feet) square and contains about one million *tesserae*. Each workshop would have had its own pattern book from which a prospective customer could choose. In the Roman world mosaics were used to decorate walls and vaults as well as floors, but in Britain it is virtually impossible to tell whether this custom was followed. One or two pieces of mosaic found in excavations hint at the possibility of wall mosaics, the most likely being a curved piece from the villa at East Malling, Kent. Walls were frequently painted and in some cases quite elaborate scenes were depicted.

Although no painted ceilings remain *in situ* in Britain, plaster recovered from excavations indicates that it was customary to paint ceiling plaster. Very occasionally a form of plaster was used to imitate architectural features such as projecting cornices or columns, and the underside of vaults was often decorated in relief with plaster (plate 33).

Plate 31. The shoulder blade of a sheep used to make bone counters found at Silchester. (Reading Museum.)

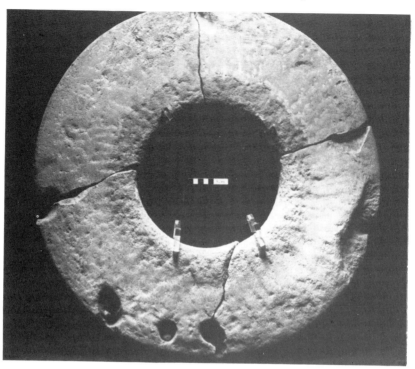

Plate 32. Flywheel about 750 millimetres (29½ inches) in diameter, made of stone, probably from a potter's wheel as illustrated in fig. 12. Found at Stibbington in a potter's workshop. (A. Challands for the Nene Valley Research Committee.)
Plate 33. Wall plaster from Verulamium. (British Museum.)

Plate 34. Fourth-century 'hare' mosaic found at Cirencester during the 1971 excavations. The materials used for mosaics usually consisted of natural stone and fired clay, but in this example decoration on the hare's back has been brought out by the use of glass. (Cirencester Excavation Committee.)

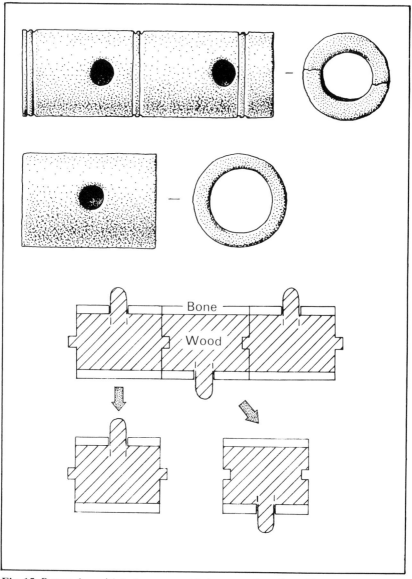

Fig. 15. Bone tubes with holes on one side have now been identified as hinges. They come in two sizes, which are illustrated at the top of the diagram, where they are drawn full size. They were joined together by pieces of wood and had wooden projections to the side. Their use as hinges is illustrated on fig. 16. (N. A. Griffiths.)

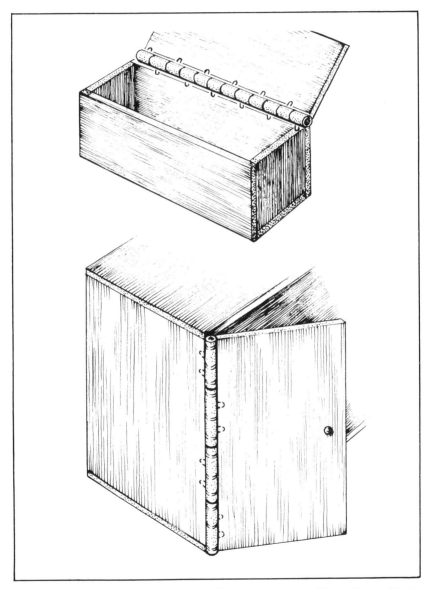

Fig. 16. A wooden chest and cupboard, illustrating the use of bone hinges. (N. A. Griffiths.)

7

Further reading

Blagg, T. F. C. 'Tools and Techniques of the Roman Stonemason in Britain', *Britannia* VII (1976), 152-72.

Brodribb, G. *Roman Brick and Tile*. Alan Sutton Publishing Ltd, 1987.

Butcher, S. A. 'Enamelling in Roman Britain', in *Studies Presented to A. J. Taylor*. London, 1974.

Cleere, H. F. 'Classification of Early Iron-Smelting Furnaces', *Antiquaries Journal,* LII (1972), 8-23.

Cleere, H. F. *The Iron Industry of the Weald*. Leicester University Press, 1985.

Crummy, N. 'A Chronology of Bone Pins', *Britannia,* X (1979), 157-63.

Davey, N., and Ling, R. *Wall-paintings in Roman Britain*. Britannia Monograph Series number 3, 1981.

Harden, D. B. 'Ancient Glass II: Roman', *Archaeological Journal,* 126 (1969), 44-77.

Higgins, R. A. *Greek and Roman Jewellery*. London, 1961.

Johnson, P. *Romano-British Mosaics*. Shire Publications, 1982.

Ling, R. *Romano-British Wall Painting*. Shire Publications, 1985.

Mackreth, D. F. *Roman Brooches*. Salisbury and South Wiltshire Museum, 1973.

McWhirr, A. D. *Roman Brick and Tile*. British Archaeological Reports S68. Oxford, 1979.

Manning, W. H. *Catalogue of the Romano-British Iron Tools, Fittings and Weapons in the British Museum*. British Museum Publications, 1986.

Neal, D. *Roman Mosaics in Britain*. Britannia Monograph Series number 1, London, 1981.

Strong, D. E. *Greek and Roman Gold and Silver Plate*. London, 1966.

Strong, D. E. *Roman Crafts*. Duckworth, 1976.

Swan, V. G. *Pottery in Roman Britain*. Shire Publications, fourth edition 1988.

Swan, V. G. *The Pottery Kilns of Roman Britain*. HMSO, 1984.

Tylecote, R. F. *Metallurgy in Archaeology*. Edward Arnold, 1962.

Wild, J. P. *Textile Manufacture in the Northern Provinces*. Cambridge University Press, 1970.

8

Monuments and museums to visit

For details of sites and museums the most comprehensive guide to Roman Britain is *A Guide to the Roman Remains in Britain* by R. J. A. Wilson (Constable and Company).

Charterhouse, Somerset (ST 5056). Little of the mining settlement can be seen today although the amphitheatre is clearly visible.

Dolaucothi, Dyfed (SN 6640). Remains of gold mines dating from the Roman period to the twentieth century. Now owned by the National Trust, which has produced a short guide to accompany three signposted walks around the mines.

Lydney, Gloucestershire (SO 6102). Entrances to Roman iron mines can be seen as well as the remains of a temple complex. It is necessary to obtain viewing permission from the Estate Office, Lydney.

Museums

Museums containing collections of Roman material usually have a wide range of objects reflecting the skills of the Roman craftsman. They include:

Bath. Roman Baths Museum, Pump Room, Stall Street.

Bristol. City Museum and Art Gallery, Queens Road, Clifton.

Cambridge. University Museum of Archaeology and Anthropology, Downing Street.

Canterbury. Royal Museum and Art Gallery, High Street.

Cardiff. National Museum of Wales, Cathays Park.

Carlisle. Museum and Art Gallery, Castle Street.

Chester. Grosvenor Museum, Grosvenor Street.

Chichester. Roman Palace and Museum, Salthill Road, Fishbourne.

Cirencester. Corinium Museum, Park Street. (A good collection of mosaics, some wall plaster and a reconstruction of a mosaicist's workshop.)

Colchester. Colchester and Essex Museum, The Castle.

Corbridge, Northumberland. Roman Site Museum.

Dorchester. Dorset County Museum, High Street West.

Dover. Roman Painted House, New Street.
Edinburgh. Royal Museum of Scotland, Queen Street.
Gloucester. City Museum and Art Gallery, Brunswick Road.
Leicester. Jewry Wall Museum of Archaeology, St Nicholas Circle.
(A growing collection of good-quality wall plaster.)
Lincoln. City and County Museum, Greyfriars, Broadgate.
London. British Museum, Great Russell Street, WC1.
Museum of London, London Wall, EC2.
Newcastle upon Tyne. Museum of Antiquities, The University.
Newport, Gwent. Museum and Art Gallery, John Frost Square.
Oxford. Ashmolean Museum of Art and Archaeology, Beaumont Street.
Peterborough. City Museum and Art Gallery, Priestgate.
Reading. Museum and Art Gallery, Blagrave Street. (A fine collection of tools and a reconstruction of a woodworker's workshop.)
St Albans. Verulamium Museum, St Michaels. (A good collection of mosaics and wall plaster and a range of tools.)
Salisbury. Salisbury and South Wiltshire Museum, The King's House, 65 The Close.
Shrewsbury. Rowley's House Museum, Barker Street.
Wall, Staffordshire. Letocetum Roman Site and Museum.
Winchester. City Museum, The Square.
Wroxeter, Shropshire. Viroconium Museum, Wroxeter Roman Site.
York. Yorkshire Museum, Museum Gardens.

Displays of wall paintings and mosaics can be seen at a number of villas laid out for the public to see. They include:

Bignor (SU 9814). Midway between the A285 and the A29 some 14 miles from Chichester. A good collection of mosaics.
Chedworth (SP 0513). Signposted off the Fosse Way (A429) in the Cotswolds. A good collection of mosaics and a range of interesting objects in the site museum.
Fishbourne (SU 8404). The palace lies about one mile to the west of Chichester and contains an important collection of mosaics and many other objects displayed in the site museum.
Lullingstone (TQ 5365). This villa is at Eynsford in Kent and can be reached by a road off the A225. There are good mosaics and wall plaster.